TABLE OF CONTENTS

MAP OF THE GAMBIA

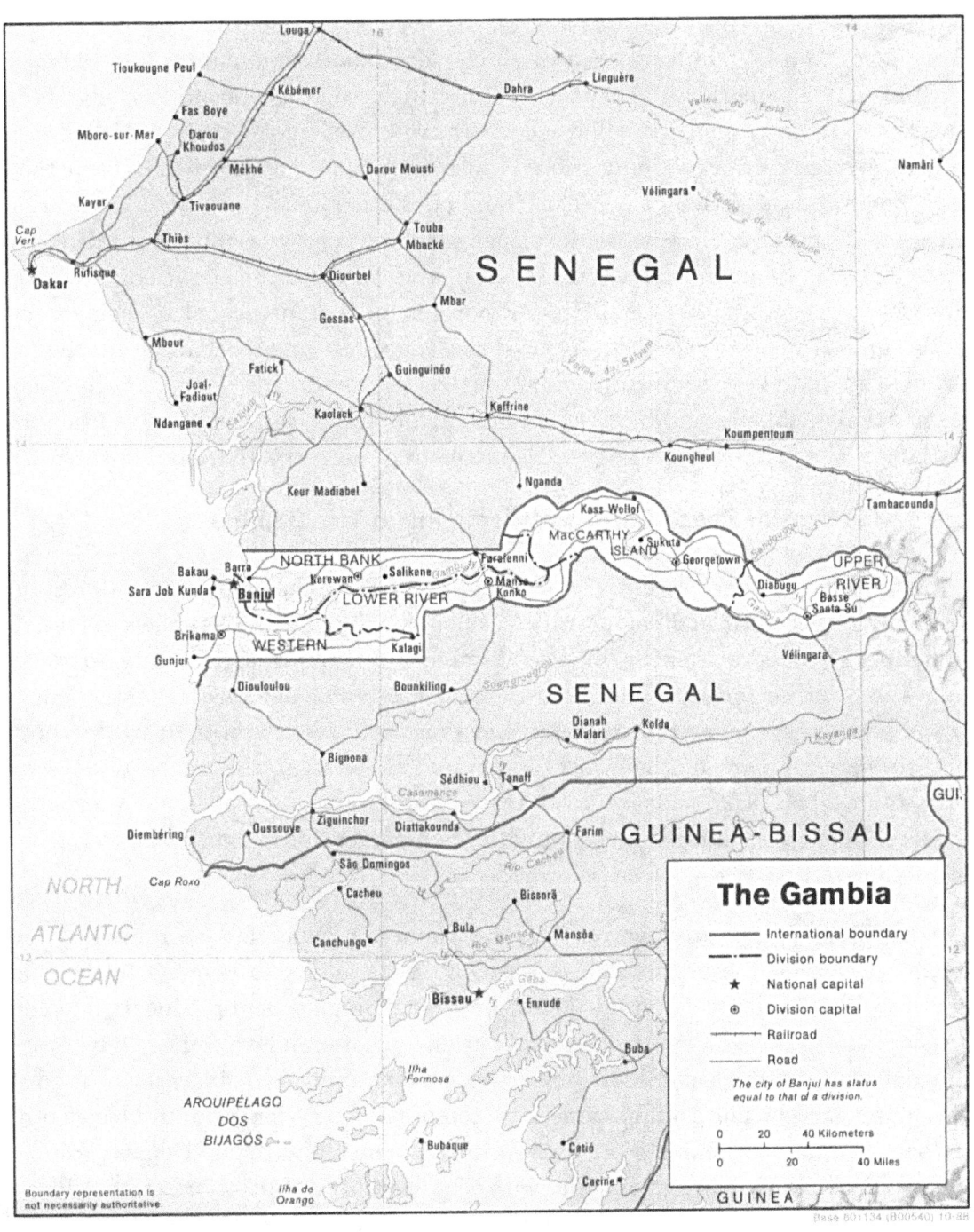

PEACE CORPS/THE GAMBIA
HISTORY AND PROGRAMS

History of the Peace Corps in The Gambia

The first Peace Corps Volunteers arrived in The Gambia at the invitation of the Gambian government in September 1967. They worked in skilled trades as mechanics, engineers, and carpenters, and they organized village cooperatives. Two years later, another group of Volunteers arrived to work in education. Since that time, education has been the main focus of Peace Corps activities in The Gambia. Education Volunteers have organized resource centers for primary schools; developed teaching curricula and materials for classes in math, science, English, and environmental and forestry conservation; and provided training for teachers in these subjects. Environment Volunteers have helped improve vegetable and fruit tree production in school gardens and orchards; helped control freshwater runoff and saltwater intrusion; constructed handmade dams that have doubled rice production; published and marketed historical narratives for the traditional Griot Society; and assisted in managing seven Department of Forestry divisional nurseries.

History and Future of Peace Corps Programming in The Gambia

Peace Corps/The Gambia currently works in three development sectors: education, the environment, and health and community development. Regardless of their sector-specific assignments, Volunteers working in The Gambia have ample opportunity to work with colleagues in other sectors, as well as in secondary activities such as HIV/AIDS education, youth and gender development, and girls' education. In the course of their work, Volunteers become an integral part of their local communities and, at the same time, have the opportunity to share U.S. culture with their host families, villages, counterparts, and supervisors. This cross-cultural understanding is as essential to the Peace Corps' mission as the technical assistance Volunteers provide.

The Peace Corps has been involved in The Gambia's education sector since 1969. A significant reason for the project's success has been its ability to respond to the changing needs of the sector over the years. In addition to teaching students, education Volunteers have assisted in the development of curricula at all educational levels. They have worked in areas ranging from vocational education to teacher training in primary school education and secondary school math and science, to computer operation and troubleshooting. In 1992, Peace Corps/The Gambia restructured its relationship with the Department of State for education to be in closer alignment with The Gambia's Education Master Plan. This plan aims to improve access to quality education for all Gambian students, especially girls.

About 30 Volunteers currently work in the **education project**. Teacher trainers conduct training for teachers at the regional and primary school levels. They also help build the capacity of their Gambian counterparts to produce and promote the use of teaching aids and student-centered learning activities, as well as help establish and manage resource centers and libraries. The rapid expansion in the number of new secondary schools, the shortage of qualified secondary school teachers (especially in math and science), the high rate of computer illiteracy, and limited information technology facilities continue to be barriers to achievement of The Gambia's development goals. To help meet these challenges, some Volunteers are providing pre-service training for teachers at Gambia College, one of two postsecondary educational institutions in the country.

The Gambia is one of Africa's smallest and least developed countries. Over the past 40 years, a combination of rapid population growth, low rainfall, unsustainable agricultural practices, and exploitation of the natural resource base, coupled with a lack of environmental awareness, has caused a dramatic decline in agricultural productivity, environmental degradation, and a loss of biodiversity.

The project plan for the **environment sector** has evolved over the years from agriculture and forestry (Volunteers in this sector are still sometimes referred to as "AgFos"). The project's purpose is to improve the quality of life of local communities by promoting protection of the environment and adoption of sustainable practices for managing natural resources. The goals are to implement practices that enable community members to manage their natural resource base (fields and forests) in a sustainable manner, to train educators working with students to increase environmental awareness and to implement activities that protect the environment, and to increase the income and improve the nutrition of rural women by educating them about horticultural techniques and nutritional practices. Volunteers use formal and nonformal education tools to promote community forestry and improved horticultural and agricultural techniques in rural communities. Environment Volunteers are also encouraged and supported in carrying out other community-based initiatives, such as beekeeping and income-generation projects for women.

About 35 Volunteers currently serve in the environment project, working in small rural communities in environmentally threatened and economically deprived areas of the country. Some Volunteers are attached to the Department of Forestry and work with community members such as government extensionists, nongovernmental organization extensionists, school teachers (for formal environmental education and school gardening), local farmers, and youth and women's groups.

About 30 Volunteers are currently serving in the heal**th and community development project**. They help develop primary health care, which The Gambia has adopted as its strategy for national health development, and they work to assess and mobilize communities for self-development. Their assignments include helping Gambians plan and deliver health education, organizing in-service training for health workers, designing teaching aids for health education, developing income-generation programs, and women and girls' empowerment activities. Volunteers in this project are also involved in enhancing the capacity of health workers and community organizations to process data and use the information for planning, problem solving, and the implementation of activities addressing identified health and community needs. Most of the health and community development Volunteers are assigned to rural areas.

COUNTRY OVERVIEW: THE GAMBIA AT A GLANCE

History

While The Gambia is continental Africa's smallest nation, its history and heritage encompass some of the continent's most significant and influential events and people. The history of The Gambia is inevitably linked to outside influences. As early as the 13th century, the area became part of the Empire of Mali, with Muslim Mandinka traders from Mali spreading into the area.

The Gambia later became a battleground between the French and the British for control of the slave trade. The country's odd shape and boundaries stem from the resolution of this conflict, as the British seized control of the Gambia River to prevent French slavers from using it as a base. The Gambia is now a narrow strip of land on either side of the lower Gambia River, which also winds through the heart of modern Senegal.

The country gained independence from Britain in 1965 and became a republic of the Commonwealth in 1970, with former Prime Minister Dawda Jawara becoming the nation's first president.

Government

The almost 30-year reign of Dawda Jawara ended on July 22, 1994, in a coup d'etat. The coup's leader was Colonel Yahya Jammeh, the former chairman of the Armed Forces Provisional Ruling Council. The military government originally set a four-year timetable for a return to civilian rule, but on the recommendation of a National Consultative Committee formed by Jammeh, this timetable was reduced to two years. Jammeh was elected president in September 1996. Jammeh's new party, the Alliance for Patriotic Reorientation and Construction, won the parliamentary elections held in January 1997, completing the country's return to democratic rule. President Jammeh has been returned to power in two successive elections, with ever-increasing majorities.

The National Assembly is also controlled by the APRC. In the villages, certain prerogatives are retained by the traditional chiefs in rural areas, who continue to play an active, though declining role in local administration and policies.

The judicial system is a combination of British common law, Islamic law, and traditional law. Most civil and criminal proceedings are under the jurisdiction of civil courts, topped by a Supreme Court. Cases that involve traditional or religious matters, such as marriage or land rights, are handled first by traditional or Islamic courts.

Economy

The Gambia is one of the least developed countries in the world, and is ranked 155 on the United Nations Development Programme's Human Development Index. On the other hand, its UNDP ranking is among the 10 most improved since the ranking began in 1975.

The agricultural sector, which employs about 75 percent of the labor force, provides seasonal employment and contributes about 22 percent to GDP.

Since the beginning of the 1990s, the tourism sector has emerged as a potential source of rapid economic growth. The Gambia's mild climate, long stretches of sandy beaches, and close proximity to Europe make it an attractive destination for European tourists. Providing both employment and foreign exchange earnings, the tourism sector accounts for between 10 and 12 percent of GDP.

The industrial sector, made up of manufacturing, construction, and utilities, is quite small and accounts for less than 10 percent of GDP. The growth of this sector is constrained by a number of factors, notably the lack of skilled personnel. Continuing shortages of utilities like electricity and water and lack of basic infrastructure also hamper growth. Finally, the sector lacks meaningful links with other sectors of the economy.

Perhaps the most rapidly growing factor in the economy is the growth in remittances from abroad, primarily England and Spain.

People and Culture

The Gambia's population is made up of five major ethnic groups, several minor ones, and a significant number of foreigners. The Mandinka make up approximately 40 percent of the people, the Fula 19 percent, the Wolof 15 percent, the Jola 10 percent, and the Serahule 9 percent. Although these groups are represented in each of the country's six administrative divisions, they are concentrated in particular areas. Mandinkas are the majority in the western half of the country, particularly in the North Bank. Wolofs are predominately in the capital, Banjul, and in some areas of the North Bank. Fulas and Serahules are largely concentrated in the east around Jangjangbureh Island and the Upper River Division, with Jolas in the Western Division. The minor ethnic groups are the Serer, Aku, and Manjago. People from other African countries and non-Africans make up the rest of the population. The country's official language is English.

Population density is around 150 people per square kilometer, making The Gambia one of the most densely populated countries in Africa. Forty percent of the population lives in urban areas. The annual population growth rate is estimated at 4.1 percent, which is attributed mainly to high adolescent fertility. The Gambia has a youthful population, with approximately 45 percent under age 15.

The Gambia's major indigenous groups have a highly stratified society in which status is determined by birth. At the top of the social ladder are traditional noble and warrior families, followed by farmers, traders, and persons of low caste, i.e., blacksmiths, leather workers, woodworkers, weavers, and griots (poets, praise singers and wandering musicians). Although griots make up the lowest caste, they are highly respected for being in charge of passing on oral traditions. Slavery did not come with the Europeans, but was a long-standing part of Gambian society. Slavery is long gone, but many descendants of former slaves still work as tenant farmers for old slave-owning families.

People in The Gambia place great importance on greetings. Wolofs and Mandinkas, for example, greet each other with a lengthy ritual that starts with the traditional Muslim greetings "Salaamu aleikum" and "Aleikum asalaam" ("Peace be with you" and "And peace be with you") and continues with questions about one another's families, home lives, villages, and health. The answers usually indicate that everything is fine and are often followed with the expression "Al hamdulillah" ("Thanks be to Allah").

Environment

More than 20 years of increasingly dry weather in the Sahel (the region south of the Sahara) has severely impacted natural resources in the area, reducing forested areas, biological diversity, and land productivity. Despite the river flowing through its center, The Gambia is no exception to the regional decrease in forested land. Tree-planting efforts in the region are estimated to be only about 10 to 15 percent of the level required to balance losses of woody vegetation due to land clearing, charcoal production, fuel collection, and brush fires. If the pattern of below-normal precipitation persists, a permanent reduction in the carrying capacity of the affected lands is probably inevitable.

RESOURCES FOR FURTHER INFORMATION

Following is a list of websites for additional information about the Peace Corps, The Gambia, and to connect you to returned Volunteers and other invitees. Please keep in mind that although we try to make sure all these links are active and current, we cannot guarantee it. If you do not have access to the Internet, visit your local library. Libraries offer free Internet usage and often let you print information to take home.

A note of caution: As you surf the Internet, be aware that you may find bulletin boards and chat rooms in which people are free to express opinions about the Peace Corps based on their own experience, including comments by those who were unhappy with their choice to serve in the Peace Corps. These opinions are not those of the Peace Corps or the U.S. government, and we hope you will keep in mind that no two people experience their service in the same way.

General Information About The Gambia

http://gamlangs.googlepages.com/

This web site, created and maintained by Volunteers, currently serving in The Gambia is your best source of information. It is more than the best place to start; it may provide all you need to know. It includes a wealth of information, photos, manuals, language lessons, and links to other useful sites-- even some Volunteer email addresses. Definitely read everything here before you go anywhere else, as it is not only current information, but is written specifically for future Volunteers.

www.countrywatch.com

On this site, you can learn anything from what time it is in the capital of The Gambia to how to convert from the dollar to the The Gambian currency. Just click on Country and go from there.

www.lonelyplanet.com/destinations

Visit this site for general travel advice about almost any country in the world.

www.state.gov

The State Department's website issues background notes periodically about countries around the world. Find The Gambia and learn more about its social and political history. You can also go to the site's international travel section to check on conditions that may affect your safety.

http://www.gambia.gm/

The official website of the government of The Gambia

http://www.africa.upenn.edu/Country_Specific/Gambia.html

This University of Pennsylvania African Studies Center website provides a comprehensive gateway to many useful online sources about The Gambia.

www.psr.keele.ac.uk/official.htm

This includes links to all the official sites for governments worldwide.

www.geography.about.com/library/maps/blindex.htm

This online world atlas includes maps and geographical information, and each country page contains links to other sites, such as the Library of Congress, that contain comprehensive historical, social, and political background.

www.cyberschoolbus.un.org/infonation/info.asp

This United Nations site allows you to search for statistical information for member states of the U.N.

www.worldinformation.com

This site provides an additional source of current and historical information about countries around the world.

Connect With Returned Volunteers and Other Invitees

www.rpcv.org

This is the site of the National Peace Corps Association, made up of returned Volunteers. On this site you can find links to all the Web pages of the "Friends of" groups for most countries of service, comprised of former Volunteers who served in those countries. There are also regional groups that frequently get together for social events and local volunteer activities.

www.PeaceCorpsWorldwide.org

This site is hosted by a group of returned Volunteer writers. It is a monthly online publication of essays and Volunteer accounts of their Peace Corps service.

http://groups.yahoo.com/group/peacecorps2

This Yahoo site hosts a bulletin board where prospective Volunteers and returned Volunteers can come together.

Recommended Books

- Hudson, Mark. *Our Grandmothers' Drums*. Grove Press, 1990. Written by a young Brit who lived for 14 months near a Gambian village, working with the women there. This is an excellent, if not perfect, introduction to Gambian village life. This book is out of print but is available through online booksellers. As close to required reading as there is.

- Burke, Andrew, and David Else. *The Gambia and Senegal: Lonely Planet*. This introduction to the cultural richness of West Africa is full of practical tips.

- Dettwyler, Katherine. *Dancing Skeletons: Life and Death in West Africa*. A personal account of a malnutrition/ anthropology study of the women and children in Mali.

- Acheba, Chinua. *Things Fall Apart*. This classic short novel of life in pre-colonial Nigeria is still relevant today to life anywhere in West Africa.

- Ba, Mariama. *So Long, a Letter*. This modern short novel by a Senegalese women's activist, is about the double standard between men and women in today's urban Africa.

Recommended Movie

- "Moolaade." The final film from African cinema's founding father, Ousmane Sembene, this is a potent polemic directed against the still-common practice of female circumcision. Set in Senegal.

Books About the History of the Peace Corps

- Hoffman, Elizabeth Cobbs. *All You Need is Love: The Peace Corps and the Spirit of the 1960s*. Cambridge, Mass.: Harvard University Press, 2000.

- Rice, Gerald T. *The Bold Experiment: JFK's Peace Corps*. Notre Dame, Ind.: University of Notre Dame Press, 1985.

- Stossel, Scott. *Sarge: The Life and Times of Sargent Shriver*. Washington, D.C.: Smithsonian Institution Press, 2004.

- Meisler, Stanley. When the World Calls: The Inside Story of the Peace Corps and its First 50 Years. Boston, Mass.: Beacon Press, 2011.

Books on the Volunteer Experience

- Dirlam, Sharon. *Beyond Siberia: Two Years in a Forgotten Place*. Santa Barbara, Calif.: McSeas Books, 2004.

- Casebolt, Marjorie DeMoss. *Margarita: A Guatemalan Peace Corps Experience*. Gig Harbor, Wash.: Red Apple Publishing, 2000.

- Erdman, Sarah. Nine Hills to Nambonkaha: Two Years in the Heart of an African Village. New York, N.Y.: Picador, 2003.

- Hessler, Peter. *River Town: Two Years on the Yangtze*. New York, N.Y.: Perennial, 2001.

- Kennedy, Geraldine ed. *From the Center of the Earth: Stories out of the Peace Corps*. Santa Monica, Calif.: Clover Park Press, 1991.

- Thompsen, Moritz. *Living Poor: A Peace Corps Chronicle*. Seattle, Wash.: University of Washington Press, 1997 (reprint).

LIVING CONDITIONS AND VOLUNTEER LIFESTYLE

Communications

The main Peace Corps office is in Fajara, near the capital city of Banjul, with an unstaffed regional sub-office in Basse (Upper River Region). There is also a transit house in which Volunteers can stay while in Fajara on business. There is electricity at all three locations, although electricity in Basse is shut off during the late night. There are four computers with Internet access at the Fajara Peace Corps office. There are Internet cafes available in large regional towns, although access times can be painfully slow.

Although The Gambia is slowly electrifying, most Volunteers are still placed in remote locations without electricity.

Mail

Few countries in the world offer the level of mail service considered normal in the United States. If you expect U.S. standards for mail service, you will be in for some frustration. Mail from the United States takes a minimum of two weeks to arrive in The Gambia, often longer. Once here, we place your mail in your mailbox at our offices. If you live outside the Fajara area, we will then deliver all mail in your mailbox to you once each month on a "mail run" in a Peace Corps vehicle. Therefore, depending on when your mail arrives and where you are posted, it could take as few as three weeks or up to seven weeks to get to you. Advise your family and friends to number their letters for tracking reasons and to include "Airmail" and "Par Avion" on their envelopes. Obviously, email is rapidly supplanting regular mail service as a means of communication.

Despite the delays, we encourage you to write to your family regularly and to number your letters. You can send mail by giving it to the Peace Corps driver when he comes on the mail run. Family members typically become worried when they do not hear from you, so it is a good idea to advise them mail service is sporadic and that they should not worry if they do not receive your letters regularly. If a serious problem were to occur, Peace Corps/The Gambia would notify the Office of Special Services at the Peace Corps headquarters in Washington, D.C., which would then contact your family.

Your address for your entire stay in the Gambia will be:

> "Your Name," PCV
> U.S. Peace Corps
> PO Box 582
> Banjul, The Gambia
> West Africa

Telephones

International phone service to and from The Gambia is fairly good, but it can be expensive. The public telephone company, Gamtel, provides service in larger towns and villages throughout the country. There are also public phone booths in smaller villages that you can use to reach an AT&T or MCI operator for international calls. Volunteers are not permitted to use the telephones at the Peace Corps office in Banjul to call family or friends unless the call pertains to an emergency and is approved in advance by the country director.

Cell phones are the preferred mode of communication in The Gambia, and all Volunteers are expected to either bring a compatible cell phone (specific standards for compatible phones are below and in the packing list) or buy a phone once in The Gambia. While landlines exist, their installation is limited due to their physical nature. Even cell phones have their coverage limits. Currently, there are three mobile service providers that cover some parts of the country very well, but most parts have limited or sporadic coverage. Because no one service has full coverage, many Volunteers even have two cell phones. As a trainee, you will be provided with more information once you arrive in-country and you will have the opportunity to purchase a mobile phone at some point during training, either during the first week in-country or at the end of training. The cheapest mobile phones in the Gambia cost anywhere from $50 to $90, depending upon the promotion. If you choose to purchase a mobile phone before departure (probably cheaper), be sure it is an unlocked quadband cell phone that takes a SIM card. A good source may be eBay or other similar sites. For a list of common cell phone models in The Gambia, please see the packing list at the end of this Welcome Book.

Computer, Internet, and Email Access

Volunteers have access to email and the Internet at the main Peace Corps office where there are four computers for Volunteer use. Volunteers generally are able to check their email at the Peace Corps offices at least once a month, but some Volunteers also have email at the schools where they teach. There are increasing numbers of private telecenters and Internet cafes in larger towns. These generally work well for email, but Internet access is both slow and expensive.

Housing and Site Location

Once you become a Volunteer, you will be provided with safe and adequate housing in accordance with the Peace Corps' site selection criteria (see the "Health Care and Safety" chapter for further information). The majority of Volunteers live in family compounds with one or two private rooms at their disposal. You will need to be very flexible in your housing expectations, as you probably will not have running water or electricity and may have to collect water from a well or borehole and spend your evenings reading by candlelight or lantern.

Peace Corps staff will visit your site periodically to provide personal, medical, and technical support.

The Peace Corps will provide you with items such as an all-terrain bicycle, mosquito net, and a water filter for use during your service.

Living Allowance and Money Management

As a Volunteer in The Gambia, you will receive several allowances. Upon being sworn in, you will receive a settling-in allowance to purchase household necessities such as a stove, dishes, a lantern, and furniture. Once you are at your site, you will receive a monthly living allowance, deposited in local currency into a Gambian bank account, to pay for daily necessities. You should be able to live adequately, albeit simply, on this allowance, which is based on an annual survey of Volunteer living costs. Living among Gambians and within their economic means is part of the Peace Corps model, but you should still have enough to set aside for travel and other expenses. In addition, a vacation allowance of $24 per month of service will be deposited along with your living allowance into your account in local currency at the beginning of every month. When visiting Peace Corps offices on official business (as approved by your program manager), or for medical reasons, you will receive a per diem allowance to cover your food and transportation.

If you bring your own money with you, U.S. dollars and traveler's checks are recommended because credit cards are not widely accepted (though they are useful for travel outside the country and cash advances). Personal checks can be cashed, but not easily, and if you think you will be doing any banking with U.S. banks, you might want to bring your checkbook. You can also have money wired from home by international bank transfer.

Food and Diet

Some Volunteers do all or some of their own cooking, but you will probably find it less expensive and more convenient to have meals with your host family. Gambians eat three meals a day, with lunch as the main meal.

In general, the rapid rise of grain prices since 2006 has put a great deal of pressure on most Gambian families, whose diet consists primarily of grains (millet, rice, etc.).

Breakfast might include a porridge made of rice, sugar, and sour milk (and sometimes pounded peanuts, a favorite among Volunteers); little balls of millet boiled in a clear, sweet, viscous liquid, which tastes better than it looks; and steamed millet (coos) meal eaten with sweetened sour milk, which may remind you of wheat germ with plain yogurt. Lunch might consist of rice topped with a tangy green sauce made of sorrel leaves, red peppers, dried fish, and onions; or rice mixed with peppers, onions, and dried fish. Typical dinner dishes are rice with a sauce of tomatoes, peppers, onions, oil, and fish, chicken, or beef; a spicy soup made of tomatoes, tomato paste, beef, potatoes, and okra and eaten over rice or coos;

and a one-pot dish of rice, tomato paste, oil, meat, and vegetables called benachin. Although most Volunteers enjoy the local food, you can get pizza, cheeseburgers, and the like when visiting Banjul.

Some foods are characteristic of certain ethnic groups or regions. If you live in a Fula community, for example, there may be a greater variety of dairy products, as their traditional occupation is cattle herding. If you live in a Wolof community, you are likely to eat more coos, while in a site near the coast, you may find a lot of fresh fish and a wider selection of fruits and vegetables.

Transportation

The Peace Corps issues bicycles to all trainees and Volunteers for use in their work assignments. For longer trips, Volunteers often use the widely available taxi and bush taxi (*gelly gelly*) service, whose fares depend on the distance and duration of the ride.

Geography and Climate

The Gambia is located in West Africa and borders the Atlantic Ocean and Senegal. It consists of two narrow strips of land on the north and south banks of the Gambia River that extend more than 200 miles into the African continent. At its widest point, The Gambia is less than 25 miles wide.

The land is almost entirely composed of the flood plain of the Gambia River, the country's most outstanding physical feature. In the west, the river's banks are thickly lined with mangrove swamps, behind which are river flats that are submerged for most of the rainy season (July to October). Sandy hills and rolling plateaus lie farther back from the river. In the east, the swamps give way to gradually ascending riverbanks backed by rolling plains, and low hills punctuate the far eastern quarter of the country. Gambia's highest point is about 170 feet above sea level. The soil quality is generally poor and subject to the damaging effects of erosion, overcultivation, and large-scale brush burning.

The predominant vegetation is Sahel savanna woodland with grass and scrub understory. There are forested areas in the west, where rainfall is the greatest. Vegetative cover has been severely affected by deforestation, fire, and cultivation, exacerbated by high population densities on arable land and traditional farming practices. While increasingly subject to exploitation, the mangrove swamps along the western half of the Gambia River have been less affected by the people's intrusion on the natural ecology.

The Gambia is a tropical country with two distinct seasons. The summer (June to September) is generally warm and humid, with an average temperature of 90 degrees Fahrenheit. The winter is dominated by dry harmattan winds from the Sahara, which give the Gambia uniquely pleasant weather, with daily sunshine and no rain. From November to May, the temperature varies between 70 F and 80 F, with a relative humidity between

30 and 60 percent. In the early and mid-1970s, The Gambia was affected by the rainfall shortages that brought the Sahel area international headlines. While total rainfall has often approached previous levels in recent years, its distribution has been erratic, causing continuing problems for the nation's rain-fed agriculture.

Social Activities

Although some Volunteers beg to differ, there will be more to do for entertainment in your village than watching your candles melt in the afternoon heat. A major part of the Peace Corps experience is socializing with the people in your community, which might include chatting while drinking tea under the shade of a large tree, attending an all-night festival, or helping the children in your host family's compound with homework. Some families may even have a TV set or a radio. You will also have plenty of time to bike, run, walk, plant a garden, or learn to play a musical instrument. Many Volunteers take advantage of their spare time to read or write. There are libraries at the Peace Corps offices in Fajara and Basse, with limited but interesting collections of books donated by past and present Volunteers. People who like to write find time to keep up with correspondence, write in their journals, or write short stories or poetry. Be sure to bring your favorite music tapes, CDs, or MP3s, which you can swap back and forth with other Volunteers. A battery-powered shortwave radio will be useful if you want to stay current on world events. The Gambia is also well suited for those who enjoy bird-watching and stargazing (with no light pollution from large cities, it is easy to spot constellations and falling stars).

Professionalism, Dress, and Behavior

Gambians attach great importance to neatness and proper dress, and Volunteers must show respect for Gambian attitudes by dressing suitably both on and off the job. When conducting official business in government or the Peace Corps offices, trainees and Volunteers are expected to wear a collared shirt or an African-style shirt, dresses, skirts, or long pants, and professional-looking shoes (i.e., no flip-flops). T-shirts are acceptable only for fieldwork. Since many of the Westerners in The Gambia are tourists, a sure way to be disrespected is to dress like one in T-shirts and sandals. Nevertheless, it is hot here, so do bring light clothes for working in the village. Everything must be washable and durable, as clothes are washed vigorously by hand and take quite a beating in the process.

Personal Safety

More detailed information about the Peace Corps' approach to safety is contained in the "Health Care and Safety" chapter, but it is an important issue and cannot be overemphasized. As stated in the Volunteer Handbook, becoming a Peace Corps Volunteer entails certain safety risks. Living and traveling in an unfamiliar environment (oftentimes alone), having a limited understanding of local language and culture, and being perceived as well-off are some of the factors that can put a Volunteer at risk. Many Volunteers experience varying degrees of unwanted attention and harassment. Petty thefts and burglaries are not uncommon, and incidents of physical and sexual assault do occur, although most Gambia Volunteers complete their two years of service without incident. The Peace Corps has established procedures and policies designed to help you reduce your risks and enhance your safety and security. These procedures and policies, in addition to safety training, will be provided once you arrive in The Gambia. Using these tools, you are expected to take responsibility for your safety and well-being.

Each staff member at the Peace Corps is committed to providing Volunteers with the support they need to successfully meet the challenges they will face to have a safe, healthy, and productive service. We encourage Volunteers and families to look at our safety and security information on the Peace Corps website at **www.peacecorps.gov/safety**.

Information on these pages gives messages on Volunteer health and Volunteer safety. There is a section titled "Safety and Security – Our Partnership." Among topics addressed are the risks of serving as a Volunteer, posts' safety support systems, and emergency planning and communications.

Rewards and Frustrations

Peace Corps service is not for everyone. Requiring greater dedication and commitment than most jobs, it is for confident, self-starting, and concerned individuals who are interested in assisting other countries and increasing human understanding across cultures.

The key to satisfying work as a Peace Corps Volunteer is the ability to establish successful human relations at all levels, which requires patience, sensitivity, and a positive professional attitude. It is essential that you work with Gambian counterparts to ensure that tasks begun during your service will continue after your departure. It is also important to realize that while you may have a lot of energy and motivation, you will be in The Gambia for only two years. Your colleagues will probably continue to work in the same job after you leave—for little money—and may not possess the same level of motivation. Often you will find yourself in situations that require the ability to motivate both yourself and your colleagues and to take action with little guidance from supervisors. You may work for months without seeing any visible impact from, and without receiving feedback on, your work. You must possess the self-confidence, patience, and vision to continue working toward long-term goals without seeing immediate results.

Nevertheless, you will have a sense of accomplishment when small projects are made effective because of your efforts. Acceptance into a foreign culture and the acquisition of a second or even a third language are also significant rewards.

Even with the many economic, social, and environmental problems confronting The Gambia today, there is an atmosphere of excitement and hope about the positive changes occurring in the country. Joining the Gambian people in their efforts at this pivotal time in their history will be both fascinating and satisfying to Volunteers who are willing to work hard, be tolerant of ambiguity, and give generously of their time. Your willingness to serve in smaller towns and villages and to give up U.S. standards of space and privacy in your living accommodations will be greatly appreciated by Gambians. Judging by the experience of former Volunteers, the peaks are well worth the difficult times, and most Volunteers leave The Gambia feeling they have gained much more than they sacrificed during their service.

How will living and working in communities affected by HIV/AIDS affect me?

The AIDS pandemic strikes across all social strata in many Peace Corps countries. The loss of teachers has crippled education systems, while illness and disability drains family income and forces governments and donors to redirect limited resources from other priorities. The fear and uncertainty AIDS causes has led to increased domestic violence and stigmatizing of people living with HIV/AIDS, isolating them from friends and family and cutting them off from economic opportunities. As a Peace Corps Volunteer, you will confront these issues on a very personal level. It is important to be aware of the high emotional toll that disease, death, and violence can have on Volunteers. As you strive to integrate into your community, you will develop relationships with local people who might die during your service. Because of the AIDS pandemic, some Volunteers will be regularly meeting with HIV-positive people and working with training staff, office staff, and host family members living with AIDS. Volunteers need to prepare themselves to embrace these relationships in a sensitive and positive manner. Likewise, malaria and malnutrition, motor vehicle accidents and other unintentional injuries, domestic violence, and corporal punishment are problems a Volunteer will have to confront in a more immediate way than is usual in the U.S. You will need to anticipate these situations and use supportive resources available throughout your training and service to maintain your own emotional strength so you can continue to be of service to your community.

Fortunately, in The Gambia, unlike many other African countries, AIDS has not yet reached pandemic proportions, and other killer diseases, notably malaria, are much more common. The official rate of HIV prevalence is about 2.8 percent, and victims are mostly concentrated in larger cities.

PEACE CORPS TRAINING

Pre-Service Training

You will need to gain the knowledge and experience necessary to successfully serve as a Volunteer in just 10 weeks. The training period will be extremely busy. It will also be a time of learning, preparation, hard work, excitement, discovery, and self-fulfillment. The effort and challenges of adapting to a new culture will draw on your reserves of patience and your sense of humor, but will be handsomely rewarded with a sense of belonging among new friends. New and difficult tasks learned will pay off in your ability to work effectively in a challenging job that will directly benefit a great number of people.

Training is competency and community-based. It emphasizes mastery of language, immersion in the culture, and the development of competencies needed to function independently as a Volunteer.

Technical Training

Technical training will prepare you to work in Gambia by building on the skills you already have and helping you develop new skills in a manner appropriate to the needs of the country. The Peace Corps staff, Gambia experts, and current Volunteers will conduct the training program. Training places great emphasis on learning how to transfer the skills you have to the community in which you will serve as a Volunteer.

Technical training will include sessions on the general economic and political environment in Gambia and strategies for working within such a framework. You will review your technical sector's goals and will meet with the Gambia agencies and organizations that invited the Peace Corps to assist them. You will be supported and evaluated throughout the training to build the confidence and skills you need to undertake your project activities and be a productive member of your community.

By the end of training, health and community development trainees will be able to contribute to the improvement of The Gambia's primary health care through the planning and implementation of educational activities that promote maternal and child health. You will also be capable of assessing and moblilizing communities to improve their own health practices. Education trainees will be ready to teach computer literacy, math and science, social and environmental studies, and/or English, as well as to implement in-service teacher-training programs. Environment trainees will be prepared to teach agroforestry and improved agricultural and horticultural techniques to rural farmers, as well as to promote community forestry projects and environmental education in schools and communities.

Language Training

As a Peace Corps Volunteer, you will find that language skills are key to personal and professional satisfaction during your service. These skills are critical to your job performance, they help you integrate into your community, and they can ease your personal adaptation to the new surroundings. Therefore, language training is at the heart of the training program. You must successfully meet minimum language requirements to complete training and become a Volunteer. Gambian language instructors teach formal language classes five days a week in small groups of four to five people.

Your language training will incorporate a community-based approach. Most of your language training will take place in small groups in a Gambian village in which the language you are learning is spoken. In addition to classroom time, you will be given assignments to work on outside of the classroom and with your host family. The goal is to get you to a point of basic social communication skills so you can practice and develop language skills further once you are at your site. Prior to being sworn in as a Volunteer, you will work on strategies to continue language studies during your service.

In order to get a head start on this vital part of your training, we encourage you to download some of the language lessons that are available at the Volunteer-created website **http://gamlangs.googlepages.com/**. Since you will want to learn greetings in all major Gambian languages, focus on those. If you want to go further with your language study, concentrate on Mandinka, since it is the language spoken by the majority of Gambians.

Cross-Cultural Training

As part of your pre-service training, you will live with a Gambian host family. This experience is designed to ease your transition to life at your site. Families go through an orientation conducted by Peace Corps staff to explain the purpose of pre-service training and to assist them in helping you adapt to living in Gambia. Many Volunteers form strong and lasting friendships with their host families.

Cross-cultural and community development training will help you improve your communication skills and understand your role as a facilitator of development. You will be exposed to topics such as community mobilization, conflict resolution, gender and development, nonformal and adult education strategies, and political structures.

Health Training

During pre-service training, you will be given basic medical training and information. You will be expected to practice preventive health care and to take responsibility for your own health by adhering to all medical policies. Trainees are required to attend all medical sessions. The topics include preventive health measures and minor and major medical issues that you might encounter while in Gambia. Nutrition, mental health, setting up a safe living compound, and how to avoid HIV/AIDS and other sexually transmitted diseases (STDs) are also covered.

Safety Training

During the safety training sessions, you will learn how to adopt a lifestyle that reduces your risks at home, at work, and during your travels. You will also learn appropriate, effective strategies for coping with unwanted attention and about your individual responsibility for promoting safety throughout your service.

Additional Trainings During Volunteer Service

In its commitment to institutionalize quality training, the Peace Corps has implemented a training system that provides Volunteers with continual opportunities to examine their commitment to Peace Corps service while increasing their technical and cross-cultural skills. During service, there are usually three training events. The titles and objectives for those trainings are as follows:

- In-service training: Provides an opportunity for Volunteers to upgrade their technical, language, and project development skills while sharing their experiences and reaffirming their commitment after having served for three to six months.

- Midterm conference (done in conjunction with technical sector in-service): Assists Volunteers in reviewing their first year, reassessing their personal and project objectives, and planning for their second year of service.

- Close-of-service conference: Prepares Volunteers for the future after Peace Corps service and reviews their respective projects and personal experiences.

The number, length, and design of these trainings are adapted to country-specific needs and conditions. The key to the training system is that training events are integrated and interrelated, from the pre-departure orientation through the end of your service, and are planned, implemented, and evaluated cooperatively by the training staff, Peace Corps staff, and Volunteers.

YOUR HEALTH CARE AND SAFETY IN THE GAMBIA

The Peace Corps' highest priority is maintaining the good health and safety of every Volunteer. Peace Corps medical programs emphasize the preventive, rather than the curative, approach to disease. The Peace Corps in Gambia maintains a clinic with a full-time medical officer, who takes care of Volunteers' primary health care needs. Additional medical services, such as testing and basic treatment, are also available in Country X at local hospitals. If you become seriously ill, you will be transported either to an American-standard medical facility in the region or to the United States.

Health Issues in The Gambia

Major health problems among Volunteers in The Gambia are uncommon and are often the result of a Volunteer not taking preventive measures to stay healthy. The most common minor health problems are ones that also exist in the United States; that is, colds, diarrhea, constipation, sinus infections, skin infections, headaches, hemorrhoids, dental problems, minor injuries, sexually transmitted diseases, adjustment disorders, emotional problems, and alcohol abuse. These problems may be more frequent or compounded by life in The Gambia because certain environmental factors raise the risk of, or exacerbate the severity of, certain illnesses and injuries.

The most common major health concerns in The Gambia are malaria, giardiasis, amoebic dysentery, and hepatitis. Because malaria is endemic in The Gambia, you are required to take antimalarial pills. In addition, you will be vaccinated to protect you against hepatitis A and B, meningitis A and C, tetanus, diphtheria, typhoid, and rabies.

Helping You Stay Healthy

The Peace Corps will provide you with all the necessary inoculations, medications, and information to stay healthy. Upon your arrival in Gambia, you will receive a medical handbook. At the end of training, you will receive a medical kit with supplies to take care of mild illnesses and first aid needs. The contents of the kit are listed later in this chapter.

During pre-service training, you will have access to basic medical supplies through the medical officer. However, you will be responsible for your own supply of prescription drugs and any other specific medical supplies you require, as the Peace Corps will not order these items during training. Please bring a three-month supply of any prescription drugs you use, since they may not be available here and it may take several months for shipments to arrive.

You will have physicals at midservice and at the end of your service. If you develop a serious medical problem during your service, the medical officer in Gambia will consult with the Office of Medical Services in Washington, D.C. If it is determined that your condition cannot be treated in Gambia, you may be sent out of the country for further evaluation and care.

Maintaining Your Health

As a Volunteer, you must accept considerable responsibility for your own health. Proper precautions will significantly reduce your risk of serious illness or injury. The adage "An ounce of prevention ..." becomes extremely important in areas where diagnostic and treatment facilities are not up to the standards of the United States. The most important of your responsibilities in Gambia is to take preventive measures as described below.

The most important step in preventing malaria, and many other tropical diseases, is to avoid mosquito and other insect bites by sleeping under a mosquito net, wearing long-sleeved tops and long pants whenever possible, using insect repellent, and making sure your windows and doors have screens.

Rabies is prevalent throughout the region, so you will receive a series of immunizations against it when you arrive in The Gambia. If you are exposed to an animal that is either known to have or suspected of having rabies, you must inform the Peace Corps medical officer at once so you can receive post-exposure booster shots.

Many illnesses that afflict Volunteers worldwide are entirely preventable if proper food and water precautions are taken. These illnesses include food poisoning, parasitic infections, hepatitis A, dysentery, Guinea worms, tapeworms, and typhoid fever. Your medical officer will discuss specific standards for water and food preparation in Gambia during pre-service training.

AIDS is less common in The Gambia than in other parts of Africa, but is more common than in the United States. Abstinence is the only certain choice for preventing infection with HIV and other sexually transmitted diseases. You are taking risks if you choose to be sexually active. To lessen risk, use a condom every time you have sex. Whether your partner is a host country citizen, a fellow Volunteer, or anyone else, do not assume this person is free of HIV/AIDS or other STDs. You will receive more information from the medical officer about this important issue.

Volunteers are expected to adhere to an effective means of birth control to prevent an unplanned pregnancy. Your medical officer can help you decide on the most appropriate method to suit your individual needs. Contraceptive methods are available without charge from the medical officer.

It is critical to your health that you promptly report to the medical office or other designated facility for scheduled immunizations, and that you let the medical officer know immediately of significant illnesses and injuries.

Women's Health Information

Pregnancy is treated in the same manner as other Volunteer health conditions that require medical attention but also have programmatic ramifications. The Peace Corps is responsible for determining the medical risk and the availability of appropriate medical care if the Volunteer remains in-country. Given the circumstances under which Volunteers live and work in Peace Corps countries, it is rare that the Peace Corps' medical and programmatic standards for continued service during pregnancy can be met.

If feminine hygiene products are not available for you to purchase on the local market, the Peace Corps medical officer in Gambia will provide them. If you require a specific product, please bring a three-month supply with you.

Your Peace Corps Medical Kit

The Peace Corps medical officer will provide you with a kit that contains basic items necessary to prevent and treat illnesses that may occur during service. Kit items can be periodically restocked at the medical office.

Medical Kit Contents

Ace bandages
Adhesive tape
American Red Cross First Aid & Safety Handbook
Antacid tablets (Tums)
Antibiotic ointment (Bacitracin/Neomycin/ Polymycin B)
Antiseptic antimicrobial skin cleaner (Hibiclens)
Band-Aids
Butterfly closures
Calamine lotion
Cepacol lozenges
Condoms

Dental floss
Diphenhydramine HCL 25 mg (Benadryl)
Insect repellent stick (Cutter's)
Iodine tablets (for water purification)
Lip balm (Chapstick)
Oral rehydration salts
Oral thermometer (Fahrenheit)
Pseudoephedrine HCL 30 mg (Sudafed)
Robitussin-DM lozenges (for cough)
Scissors
Sterile gauze pads
Tetrahydrozaline eyedrops (Visine)
Tinactin (antifungal cream)
Tweezers

Before You Leave: A Medical Checklist

If there has been any change in your health – physical, mental, or dental – since you submitted your examination reports to the Peace Corps, you must immediately notify the Office of Medical Services. Failure to disclose new illnesses, injuries, allergies, or pregnancy can endanger your health and may jeopardize your eligibility to serve.

If your dental exam was done more than a year ago, or if your physical exam is more than two years old, contact the Office of Medical Services to find out whether you need to update your records. If your dentist or Peace Corps dental consultant has recommended that you undergo dental treatment or repair, you must complete that work and make sure your dentist sends requested confirmation reports or X-rays to the Office of Medical Services.

If you wish to avoid having duplicate vaccinations, contact your physician's office to obtain a copy of your immunization record and bring it to your pre-departure orientation. If you have any immunizations prior to Peace Corps service, the Peace Corps cannot reimburse you for the cost. The Peace Corps will provide all the immunizations necessary for your overseas assignment, either at your pre-departure orientation or shortly after you arrive in Gambia. You do not need to begin taking malaria medication prior to departure.

Bring a three-month supply of any prescription or over-the-counter medication you use on a regular basis, including birth control pills. Although the Peace Corps cannot reimburse you for this three-month supply, it will order refills during your service. While awaiting shipment – which can take several months – you will be dependent on your own medication supply. The Peace Corps will not pay for herbal or nonprescribed medications, such as St. John's wort, glucosamine, selenium, or antioxidant supplements.

You are encouraged to bring copies of medical prescriptions signed by your physician. This is not a requirement, but they might come in handy if you are questioned in transit about carrying a three-month supply of prescription drugs.

If you wear eyeglasses, bring two pairs with you – a pair and a spare. If a pair breaks, the Peace Corps will replace them, using the information your doctor in the United States provided on the eyeglasses form during your examination. The Peace Corps discourages you from using contact lenses during your service to reduce your risk of developing a serious infection or other eye disease. Most Peace Corps countries do not have appropriate water and sanitation to support eye care with the use of contact lenses. The Peace Corps will not supply or replace contact lenses or associated solutions unless an ophthalmologist has recommended their use for a specific medical condition and the Peace Corps' Office of Medical Services has given approval.

If you are eligible for Medicare, are over 50 years of age, or have a health condition that may restrict your future participation in health care plans, you may wish to consult an insurance specialist about unique coverage needs before your departure. The Peace Corps will provide all necessary health care from the time you leave for your pre-departure orientation until you complete your service. When you finish, you will be entitled to the post-service health care benefits described in the Peace Corps Volunteer Handbook. You may wish to consider keeping an existing health plan in effect during your service if you think age or pre-existing conditions might prevent you from re-enrolling in your current plan when you return home.

SAFETY AND SECURITY: OUR PARTNERSHIP

Serving as a Volunteer overseas entails certain safety and security risks. Living and traveling in an unfamiliar environment, a limited understanding of the local language and culture, and the perception of being a wealthy American are some of the factors that can put a Volunteer at risk. Property theft and burglaries are not uncommon. Incidents of physical and sexual assault do occur, although almost all Volunteers complete their two years of service without serious personal safety problems.

Beyond knowing that Peace Corps approaches safety and security as a partnership with you, it might be helpful to see how this partnership works. Peace Corps has policies, procedures, and training in place to promote your safety. We depend on you to follow those policies and to put into practice what you have learned. An example of how this works in practice – in this case to help manage the risk of burglary – is:

- Peace Corps assesses the security environment where you will live and work
- Peace Corps inspects the house where you will live according to established security criteria
- Peace Corps provides you with resources to take measures such as installing new locks
- Peace Corps ensures you are welcomed by host country authorities in your new community
- Peace Corps responds to security concerns that you raise
- You lock your doors and windows
- You adopt a lifestyle appropriate to the community where you live
- You get to know neighbors
- You decide if purchasing personal articles insurance is appropriate for you
- You don't change residences before being authorized by Peace Corps
- You communicate concerns that you have to Peace Corps staff

Factors that Contribute to Volunteer Risk

There are several factors that can heighten a Volunteer's risk, many of which are within the Volunteer's control. By far the most common crime that Volunteers experience is theft. Thefts often occur when Volunteers are away from their sites, in crowded locations (such as markets or on public transportation), and when leaving items unattended.

Before you depart for Gambia there are several measures you can take to reduce your risk:

- Leave valuable objects in the U.S.

- Leave copies of important documents and account numbers with someone you trust in the U.S.

- Purchase a hidden money pouch or "dummy" wallet as a decoy

- Purchase personal articles insurance

After you arrive in Gambia, you will receive more detailed information about common crimes, factors that contribute to Volunteer risk, and local strategies to reduce that risk. For example, Volunteers in Gambia learn to:

- Choose safe routes and times for travel, and travel with someone trusted by the community whenever possible

- Make sure one's personal appearance is respectful of local customs

- Avoid high-crime areas

- Know the local language to get help in an emergency

- Make friends with local people who are respected in the community

- Limit alcohol consumption

As you can see from this list, you must be willing to work hard and adapt your lifestyle to minimize the potential for being a target for crime. As with anywhere in the world, crime does exist in the Gambia. You can reduce your risk by avoiding situations that place you at risk and by taking precautions. Crime at the village or town level is less frequent than in the large cities; people know each other and generally are less likely to steal from their neighbors. Tourist attractions in large towns are favorite worksites for pickpockets.

Risk factors can vary within countries throughout the world that are served by the Peace Corps. A Volunteer in The Gambia may face risks specific to this country in addition to risks associated with living in a developing country.

Perhaps the single greatest risk to your safety in the Gambia is public transportation. While public buses, taxis, and private vehicles are generally safe, many accidents occur in "bush taxis." Bush taxis are the main mode of transport for Gambians and may be the only type of local transportation available to and from your community. Because of bad roads, poor auto maintenance, and overloading, bush taxis are prone to breakdowns. During the rainy season, road conditions deteriorate and accidents are even more frequent. To minimize these risks, Volunteers are encouraged not to travel at night.

The ongoing civil war in the Casamance region of southern Senegal (which began in the early 1980s) has not directly affected Volunteers serving in The Gambia. Although the region is off-limits to Volunteers, heightened awareness near the southwestern Gambia-Senegal border is warranted.

In the coastal areas, where tourists congregate, Volunteers are often mistaken for Europeans on vacation, and this assumption can bring with it preconceived notions about personal wealth or sexual mores. (A small but noticeable number of tourists are "sex tourists" who come here to rent a companion for their time in country; most of these are older European women coming to hire young Gambian men.) So young men, referred to as "bumsters," may offer to help you or "be your friend." These men are usually harmless, but they are annoying and can sometimes be aggressive. Once again, command of the local language, visiting the beach in a group, and being aware of your environment are key in decreasing your risk.

Volunteers, as well as tourists and other expatriates, are often referred to as *toubab*, which is not a derogatory term but merely means "stranger," "outsider," or, sometimes, "white person" (literally, it means from across the sea).

Any nonmedical issues involving personal security, such as those related to housing and transportation, should be directed to the safety and security coordinator.

While whistles and exclamations may be fairly common on the street, this behavior can be reduced if you dress conservatively, abide by local cultural norms, and respond according to the training you will receive.

Staying Safe: Don't Be a Target for Crime

You must be prepared to take on a large degree of responsibility for your own safety. You can make yourself less of a target, ensure that your home is secure, and develop relationships in your community that will make you an unlikely victim of crime. While the factors that contribute to your risk in Gambia may be different, in many ways you can do what you would do if you moved to a new city anywhere: Be cautious, check things out, ask questions, learn about your neighborhood, know where the more risky locations are, use common sense, and be aware. You can reduce your vulnerability to crime by integrating into your community, learning the local language, acting responsibly, and abiding by Peace Corps policies and procedures. Serving safely and effectively in Gambia will require that you accept some restrictions on your current lifestyle.

Support from Staff

If a trainee or Volunteer is the victim of a safety incident, Peace Corps staff is prepared to provide support. All Peace Corps posts have procedures in place to respond to incidents of crime committed against Volunteers. The first priority for all posts in the aftermath of an incident is to ensure the Volunteer is safe and receiving medical treatment as needed. After assuring the safety of the Volunteer, Peace Corps staff response may include reassessing the Volunteer's worksite and housing arrangements and making any adjustments, as needed. In some cases, the nature of the incident may necessitate a site or housing transfer. Peace Corps staff will also assist Volunteers with preserving their rights to pursue legal sanctions against the perpetrators of the crime. It is very important that Volunteers report incidents as they occur, not only to protect their peer Volunteers, but also to preserve the future right to prosecute. Should Volunteers decide later in the process that they want to proceed with the prosecution of their assailant, this option may no longer exist if the evidence of the event has not been preserved at the time of the incident.

Crime Data for Gambia

Crime data and statistics for Gambia, which is updated yearly, are available at the following link: **http://www.peacecorps.gov/countrydata/gambia**.

Few Peace Corps Volunteers are victims of serious crimes and crimes that do occur overseas are investigated and prosecuted by local authorities through the local courts system. If you are the victim of a crime, you will decide if you wish to pursue prosecution. If you decide to prosecute, Peace Corps will be there to assist you. One of our tasks is to ensure you are fully informed of your options and understand how the local legal process works. Peace Corps will help you ensure your rights are protected to the fullest extent possible under the laws of the country.

If you are the victim of a serious crime, you will learn how to get to a safe location as quickly as possible and contact your Peace Corps office. It's important that you notify Peace Corps as soon as you can so Peace Corps can provide you with the help you need.

Volunteer Safety Support in Gambia

The Peace Corps' approach to safety is a five-pronged plan to help you stay safe during your service and includes the following: information sharing, Volunteer training, site selection criteria, a detailed emergency action plan, and protocols for addressing safety and security incidents. Gambia's in-country safety program is outlined below.

The Peace Corps/Gambia office will keep you informed of any issues that may impact Volunteer safety through **information sharing**. Regular updates will be provided in Volunteer newsletters and in memorandums from the country director. In the event of a critical situation or emergency, you will be contacted through the emergency communication network. An important component of the capacity of Peace Corps to keep you informed is your buy-in to the partnership concept with the Peace Corps staff. It is expected that you will do your part in ensuring that Peace Corps staff members are kept apprised of your movements in-country so they are able to inform you.

Volunteer training will include sessions on specific safety and security issues in Gambia. This training will prepare you to adopt a culturally appropriate lifestyle and exercise judgment that promotes safety and reduces risk in your home, at work, and while traveling. Safety training is offered throughout service and is integrated into the language, cross-cultural aspects, health, and other components of training. You will be expected to successfully complete all training competencies in a variety of areas, including safety and security, as a condition of service.

Certain **site selection criteria** are used to determine safe housing for Volunteers before their arrival. The Peace Corps staff works closely with host communities and counterpart agencies to help prepare them for a Volunteer's arrival and to establish expectations of their respective roles in supporting the Volunteer. Each site is inspected before the Volunteer's arrival to ensure placement in appropriate, safe, and secure housing and worksites. Site selection is based, in part, on any relevant site history; access to medical, banking, postal, and other essential services; availability of communications, transportation, and markets; different housing options and living arrangements; and other Volunteer support needs.

You will also learn about Peace Corps/Gambia's **detailed emergency action plan**, which is implemented in the event of civil or political unrest or a natural disaster. When you arrive at your site, you will complete and submit a site locator form with your address, contact information, and a map to your house. If there is a security threat, you will gather with other Volunteers in Gambia at predetermined locations until the situation is resolved or the Peace Corps decides to evacuate.

Finally, in order for the Peace Corps to be fully responsive to the needs of Volunteers, it is imperative that Volunteers immediately report any security incident to the Peace Corps office. The Peace Corps has established protocols for **addressing safety and security incidents** in a timely and appropriate manner, and it collects and evaluates safety and security data to track trends and develop strategies to minimize risks to future Volunteers.

DIVERSITY AND CROSS-CULTURAL ISSUES

In fulfilling its mandate to share the face of America with host countries, the Peace Corps is making special efforts to assure that all of America's richness is reflected in the Volunteer corps. More Americans of color are serving in today's Peace Corps than at any time in recent history. Differences in race, ethnic background, age, religion, and sexual orientation are expected and welcomed among our Volunteers. Part of the Peace Corps' mission is to help dispel any notion that Americans are all of one origin or race and to establish that each of us is as thoroughly American as the other despite our many differences.

Our diversity helps us accomplish that goal. In other ways, however, it poses challenges. In Gambia, as in other Peace Corps host countries, Volunteers' behavior, lifestyle, background, and beliefs are judged in a cultural context very different from their own. Certain personal perspectives or characteristics commonly accepted in the United States may be quite uncommon, unacceptable, or even repressed in Gambia.

Outside of Gambia's capital, residents of rural communities have had relatively little direct exposure to other cultures, races, religions, and lifestyles. What people view as typical American behavior or norms may be a misconception, such as the belief that all Americans are rich and have blond hair and blue eyes. The people of Gambia are justly known for their generous hospitality to foreigners; however, members of the community in which you will live may display a range of reactions to cultural differences that you present.

To ease the transition and adapt to life in Gambia, you may need to make some temporary, yet fundamental compromises in how you present yourself as an American and as an individual. For example, female trainees and Volunteers may not be able to exercise the independence available to them in the United States; political discussions need to be handled with great care; and some of your personal beliefs may best remain undisclosed. You will need to develop techniques and personal strategies for coping with these and other limitations. The Peace Corps staff will lead diversity and sensitivity discussions during pre-service training and will be on call to provide support, but the challenge ultimately will be your own.

Overview of Diversity in Gambia

The Peace Corps staff in Gambia recognizes the adjustment issues that come with diversity and will endeavor to provide support and guidance. During pre-service training, several sessions will be held to discuss diversity and coping mechanisms. We look forward to having male and female Volunteers from a variety of races, ethnic groups, ages, religions, and sexual orientations, and hope that you will become part of a diverse group of Americans who take pride in supporting one another and demonstrating the richness of American culture.

What Might a Volunteer Face?

Possible Issues for Female Volunteers

Gambian women, especially in rural areas, have very traditional roles. As a result, North American women may not be able to exercise the freedoms to which they are accustomed. In addition, it is common for women to receive stares, comments, and requests for dates or sex. Female Volunteers develop a variety of creative strategies to handle these situations (as do male Volunteers who do not conform to the machismo image expected of them).

Possible Issues for Volunteers of Color

Gambians may expect African-American Volunteers to learn languages and adapt to the culture quicker than other Volunteers. African Americans may also sometimes be mistaken as Africans and may experience impatience on the part of Gambians when they do not demonstrate expected behavior. Asian, Arab, and Hispanic Americans may also be associated with their ancestral origins rather than their American nationality. It is helpful to remember that these reactions come from a simple lack of understanding and that they afford an opportunity to tell Gambians more about the diversity of America. From time to time, Volunteers of color may even feel some isolation within the Volunteer community because some Volunteers may lack knowledge of diversity issues in the United States.

Volunteer Comment

"Overall, my work-related and social experiences as an African-American Volunteer in The Gambia have been very positive. At work, I've been judged by my personality, my level of professionalism, and my skills, not by my color. This is quite different from what I encountered back home for most of my life.

"There are days when I'm hardly recognized as a non-Gambian. There are other days—when I do not have my natural dreadlocks covered or when I'm not wearing traditional Gambian clothes—when I stick out like a sore thumb. Those are my most challenging days. I've found that when people cannot really label me as being entirely African or entirely American, they may interact with me with mixed emotions. On the one hand, because you are black you may be considered and respected as part of the family but from another ethnic group (or from the same ethnic group but from another country). On the other hand, because you are black and come from America, you may be expected to give more (like money or favors). Some people may be highly offended when you put up personal boundaries, believing that you think you are 'better than they' or that you are a 'useless toubab' (non-Gambian person).

"The people you grow really close to, however, are those who have come to know who you are as an individual, thereby respecting and valuing your differences."

Possible Issues for Senior Volunteers

Older individuals are highly respected in The Gambia, which is certainly a plus. But with this respect comes the expectation that senior Volunteers will have relatively more knowledge and experience. Because acquisition of a new language is often more difficult for seniors, they may become frustrated with difficulties in communicating ideas important to them and may need to be assertive in developing an effective individual approach to language learning. In addition, some older Volunteers find pre-service training to be physically challenging.

Because the vast majority of Volunteers in The Gambia are young, older Volunteers sometimes feel isolated within the Volunteer community. Peace Corps/The Gambia is sensitive to this issue and takes it into consideration when placing senior Volunteers. Seniors sometimes are sought out by younger members of the Volunteer community for advice, and while some enjoy the role of mentor, others would rather not fulfill this role.

Possible Issues for Gay, Lesbian, or Bisexual Volunteers

The Gambia is conservative by U.S. standards, and many Gambians disapprove of homosexuality. There were recently riots in Senegal after two men held a public wedding, and the president of The Gambia has publicly stated that gays are not welcome in the country. (This is typical of conservative Muslim countries.) Because of this, gay, lesbian, and bisexual Volunteers have not been able to be open about their sexual orientation. However, Peace Corps/The Gambia provides an open and supportive atmosphere for gay, lesbian, and bisexual Volunteers, and there is an informal mutual-support organization of Volunteers that meets periodically.

A recommended resource for support and advice prior to and during your service is the Lesbian, Gay, Bisexual & Transgender U.S. Peace Corps Alumni website at **www.lgbrpcv.org**.

Possible Religious Issues for Volunteers

The Gambia is overwhelmingly Muslim, with a small Christian minority. Although most Gambians have little knowledge of other religions, there is a high degree of religious tolerance in the country. Occasionally, a Gambian friend may encourage you to explore or convert to Islam.

Possible Issues for Volunteers With Disabilities

As part of the medical clearance process, the Peace Corps Office of Medical Services determined that you were physically and emotionally capable, with or without reasonable accommodations, to perform a full tour of Volunteer service in Gambia without unreasonable risk of harm to yourself or interruption of service. The Peace Corps/ Gambia staff will work with disabled Volunteers to make reasonable accommodations for them in training, housing, jobsites, or other areas to enable them to serve safely and effectively.

The accommodations that make life more manageable for those with disabilities in the United States are absent in The Gambia, so certain aspects of everyday life can be extremely difficult. Nevertheless, Gambians are very accepting of people with disabilities.

FREQUENTLY ASKED QUESTIONS

This list has been compiled by Volunteers serving in The Gambia and is based on their experience. Use it as an informal guide in making your own list, bearing in mind that each experience is individual. There is no perfect list! You obviously cannot bring everything on the list, so consider those items that make the most sense to you personally and professionally. You can always have things sent to you later. As you decide what to bring, keep in mind that you have a 100-pound weight limit on baggage. And remember, you can get almost everything you need in The Gambia.

How much luggage am I allowed to bring to Gambia?

Most airlines have baggage size and weight limits and assess charges for transport of baggage that exceeds those limits. The Peace Corps has its own size and weight limits and will not pay the cost of transport for baggage that exceeds these limits. The Peace Corps' allowance is two checked pieces of luggage with combined dimensions of both pieces not to exceed 107 inches (length + width + height) and a carry-on bag with dimensions of no more than 45 inches. Checked baggage should not exceed 100 pounds total with a maximum weight of 50 pounds for any one bag.

Peace Corps Volunteers are not allowed to take pets, weapons, explosives, radio transmitters (shortwave radios are permitted), automobiles, or motorcycles to their overseas assignments. Do not pack flammable materials or liquids such as lighter fluid, cleaning solvents, hair spray, or aerosol containers. This is an important safety precaution.

What is the electric current in Gambia?

The electric current is 220 volts, but electricity is extremely irregular outside Banjul and in rural areas.

How much money should I bring?

Volunteers are expected to live at the same level as the people in their community. You will be given a settling-in allowance and a monthly living allowance, which should cover your expenses. Volunteers often wish to bring additional money for vacation travel to other countries. Credit cards and traveler's checks are preferable to cash. If you choose to bring extra money, bring the amount that will suit your own travel plans and needs.

When can I take vacation and have people visit me?

Each Volunteer accrues two vacation days per month of service (excluding training). Leave may not be taken during training, the first three months of service, or the last three months of service, except in conjunction with an authorized emergency leave. Family and friends are welcome to visit you after pre-service training and the first three months of service as long as their stay does not interfere with your work. Extended stays at your site are not encouraged and may require permission from your country director. The Peace Corps is not able to provide your visitors with visa, medical, or travel assistance.

Will my belongings be covered by insurance?

The Peace Corps does not provide insurance coverage for personal effects; Volunteers are ultimately responsible for the safekeeping of their personal belongings. However, you can purchase personal property insurance before you leave. If you wish, you may contact your own insurance company; additionally, insurance application forms will be provided, and we encourage you to consider them carefully. Volunteers should not ship or take valuable items overseas. Jewelry, watches, radios, cameras, and expensive appliances are subject to loss, theft, and breakage, and in many places, satisfactory maintenance and repair services are not available. The Peace Corps does provide a safe in which travelers checks, extra dollars, passports, and other documents can be stored.

Do I need an international driver's license?

Volunteers in the Gambia do not need an international driver's license because they are prohibited from operating privately owned motorized vehicles. Most urban travel is by bus or taxi. Rural travel ranges from buses and minibuses to trucks, bicycles, and lots of walking. On very rare occasions, a Volunteer may be asked to drive a sponsor's vehicle, but this can occur only with prior written permission from the country director. Should this occur, the Volunteer may obtain a local driver's license. A U.S. driver's license will facilitate the process, so bring it with you just in case.

What should I bring as gifts for Country X friends and my host family?

This is not a requirement. A token of friendship is sufficient. Some gift suggestions include knickknacks for the house; pictures, books, or calendars of American scenes; souvenirs from your area; hard candies that will not melt or spoil; or photos to give away.

Where will my site assignment be when I finish training and how isolated will I be?

Peace Corps trainees are not assigned to individual sites until after they have completed pre-service training. This gives Peace Corps staff the opportunity to assess each trainee's technical and language skills prior to assigning sites, in addition to finalizing site selections with their ministry counterparts. If feasible, you may have the opportunity to provide input on your site preferences, including geographical location, distance from other Volunteers, and living conditions. However, keep in mind that many factors influence the site selection process and that the Peace Corps cannot guarantee placement where you would ideally like to be. Most Volunteers live in small towns or in rural villages and are usually within one hour from another Volunteer. Some sites require a 10- to 12-hour drive from the capital. There is at least one Volunteer based in each of the regional capitals and about five to eight Volunteers in the capital city.

How can my family contact me in an emergency?

The Peace Corps' Office of Special Services (OSS) provides assistance in handling emergencies affecting trainees and Volunteers or their families. Before leaving the United States, instruct your family to notify the Office of Special Services immediately if an emergency arises, such as a serious illness or death of a family member. During normal business hours, the number for the Office of Special Services is 855.855.1961, then select option 2; or directly at 202-692-1470. After normal business hours and on weekends and holidays, the OSS duty officer can be reached at the above number. For non-emergency questions, your family can get information from your country desk staff at the Peace Corps by calling 855.855.1961.

Can I call home from The Gambia?

You will be able to call home on your cellphone, if you sign up for international service. International calls can also be made from Banjul and most larger towns, but telephone service is expensive and is not always reliable.

Should I bring a cellular phone with me?

Differences in technology make most U.S. cellular phones incompatible with the cellular service in The Gambia. You can purchase a cellphone locally, but they may cost a bit more than the equivalent in the U.S. As a trainee, you will be provided with more information once you arrive in-country and you will have the opportunity to purchase mobiles at some point during training, either during the first week in-country or at the end of training. If you want to purchase a phone in the U.S., make sure it is a Quad-Band GSM phone and is unlocked. Advanced features, such as sending and receiving pictures, and Internet access, are not useful. Your phone will be used mainly for texting, and also for voice calls.

Will there be email and Internet access? Should I bring my computer?

Because the availability of electricity is so sporadic in the rural areas where most Volunteers live, most Volunteers do not bring their own computer. Volunteers have access to email and the Internet at the main Peace Corps office and some Volunteers also have access to email at the schools where they teach. That said, some Volunteers have found having a laptop to be useful.

Electricity in The Gambia is mostly limited to the area around the capital, Banjul. However, some large towns elsewhere in the country do have electricity for several hours a day. Some organizations, such as health centers and NGOs, also have diesel generators. Regardless, a Volunteer should NOT expect to have any access to electricity, even if your posting is in the area around the capital. Electricity service, while fairly dependable in recent months, still invariably encounters problems that leave vast areas without power, sometimes for days and weeks. A Volunteer coming to The Gambia should take this into account when deciding what kind of technologies to bring along.

Having said that, a fair number of Volunteers, particularly Education-ICT Volunteers, use such things as computer laptops in The Gambia on a daily basis, since their postings tend to be associated with organizations that have access to a diesel generator. Furthermore, many non-ICT Volunteers, even those posted up-country, in rural villages, also possess similar technologies, as one can usually find a way to charge laptops, portable DVD players, cell phones and iPods, even if it requires biking a considerable distance. The Peace Corps office has four computers connected to the Internet for Volunteer use. There can be a considerable wait for these on the last weekend of the month (when Volunteers come to town to do their banking). Peace Corps also has a wireless hotspot in the office for those who bring their own laptop.

Before packing any electronics, consider the effect of high humidity on the technologies you bring. Humidity during the rainy season can cause long-term problems in sensitive devices such as laptops and iPods; however, this has not been a major concern for Volunteers who possess such technologies in The Gambia. Some preventive measures can be taken to ensure it does not become a problem.

Also, do not bring any piece of technology you would be devastated to lose. In addition to the environmental wear-and-tear, cell phones, iPods, and laptops are prime targets for theft. We encourage you to take out personal property insurance on any item of value, as the Peace Corps is not responsible for reimbursement in the case of damage or loss of these items.

WELCOME LETTERS FROM COUNTRY VOLUNTEERS

Rules of the Road:

1) Have an open mind.

FAQ's: What? Have an open mind, that's it? Did you think I'd come here without an open mind?

Before staging I told myself that the most valuable tool I would need to adjust to working in The Gambia was to stay open-minded to the culture; being sensitive to issues I'd encounter in order to effectively promote development and a positive image for the Peace Corps. I was probably right, but I didn't have any experience to back up that statement. In other words, I didn't know what I was talking about. I completely underestimated the depth of that thought and didn't understand the type of work it entailed.

Working in The Gambia requires a lot of patience, critical thinking, and personal initiative. Being open-minded not only refers to an approach for understanding and integrating in a foreign culture, but it also refers to the creative adaptation of skills and work experience you've acquired to successfully achieve your primary goal in development work: sustainability.

You're going to be here for two years, which is a lot of time to learn about sustainable development in The Gambia. You'll probably be amazed at how helpful basic skills you learned in school can be utilized in the community you're posted in. But don't jump into things right away; take some time to learn the culture and figure out a way to properly integrate your skills into their culture. In many ways I feel that my main job here is to transfer knowledge; but my work is ineffective if I don't act in a way that is culturally meaningful, in other words, in a way they will embrace, that will be sustainable.

Expect to be challenged continuously. A lot of Gambians are curious about your life in the U.S. and about our government's policies. Many of these people are poorly educated or have very little access to media resources, which can make these encounters frustrating. In my experience, Gambians have a very "in-your-face" culture, so expect to frequently receive silly questions and forward accusations about anything Western. It takes a lot of patience at first, but after awhile you'll learn their cultural norms and be able to respond to them with the terms and in the manner they can effectively understand. Look at those challenges as a practicing arena for communicating to Gambians and apply what you've learned when you create your development plans.

It is very likely that your development plans are going to change, that's another reason to stay open-minded. Many Volunteers are responsible for creating their own work plans, which you can expect to be continually fine-tuning. Development work is as much a learning process for the community as it is for the Volunteer. I remember being frustrated with the Peace Corps before I came in-country because they hadn't provided me with a job description of my two-year service. That's because there is no description. It's my service.

2) See rule #1 (Get it? Ha!)

~ Frank Ibarra, Environment Volunteer

Bissimaliah! Welcome to The Gambia. Slip off your sandals, step inside the mud hut and have a seat on one of the two sagging beds. Do you have peace? How is the family? How is the morning? In only a few months you'll be as comfortable with the etiquette for visiting and greeting Gambians as you now are with saying "hey" as you pass an acquaintance on the street.

If you allow it, your next two years in The Gambia will be the ultimate cultural experience. Learning how to carry water on your head, how to farm with a short-handled hoe, how to dance at a naming ceremony and how to pound grain with a giant wooden mortar and pestle was just the beginning for me. I was welcomed into the very heart of a host family in a small rural village. As a result of having this access, yet being a foreigner, I often felt awkward, misunderstood and scrutinized. Eventually my language skills improved, I came up with funny retorts and I began to enjoy being in the spotlight. To be happy in such a different culture, you will frequently re-adjust your expectations of yourself, of your community, or your counterpart, and even of perfect strangers.

The Gambia is a place to learn the value of "being" as opposed to "doing." Spending time with people and letting yourself be known is how you earn people's trust and, in turn, decide if you want to work with them. I consider myself a freelance roaming Agfo, open to working with anyone who is already motivated. I've taught individuals how to graft mangoes, process beeswax, make soap, and plant bananas. I started environmental clubs at local elementary schools and I connected my village development committee with a soy multiplication project. I've noted the benefits of cashews in every conversation I've had with farmers about the low price of groundnuts. As the national coordinator for a school tree nursery competition, I've stood in the dusty field behind my compound text messaging my counterparts at the Department of Forestry, the National Environment Agency, and the Department of Education. I've written letters outlining the collaboration between our institutions, approached a dozen NGOs for funding, and submitted articles to the national newspaper for the tree nursery competition.

In the end, though, the most satisfying moments of my Peace Corps experience are in my village when my favorite toddler squeals my name and races to hug my knees, when my sister's impersonation of my brother reduces me to tears of laughter, and when my family includes me as one of their own in the ceremony for giving our daughter to her new husband. Nothing can quite prepare you for the ups and downs of life in Peace Corps/The Gambia, but actually, that is exactly why you are coming here--to experience it.

~ Sarah Lee, Environment Volunteer

In the Gambia, every day is an adventure. It's hard to know what to expect when you step out of your hut in the morning, even if you have plans. On an ordinary day, if you can call it that, you may find yourself doing a little work on three different projects, helping your family through their everyday chores, meeting new people, and being perplexed by yet another local custom or cultural practice. It can be very hard to plan things here, which requires you to be flexible and resourceful when it comes to getting things done.

Each day I awaken early and do the daily morning routine. Opening my door and greeting my family itself can take 20 minutes. Gambian families tend to be large and most of them will be up before you. While collecting water, washing, watering the garden, and preparing breakfast, I try to think about what I would like to work on for the day. Some days it's a reproductive and child health clinic, sometimes it's a long day in the garden or possibly a trip to a nearby village to chat with the women about proper nutrition and other topics. Possibly, I will spend the whole day around the compound with the family, playing with the boys, sharing gardening tips with my host mothers, or going out to collect firewood with the men. Oftentimes a friend will come by to greet me, never with any warning. But greetings are very important in Gambian society, so the work comes to a halt as I offer my friend a drink and sit with him or her to chat for a while. Mothers from nearby compounds visit often to pick Moringa leaves from my backyard, which they will use to make an herbal tea that is high in vitamins. This can lead to an impromptu health talk, a follow-up trip to teach them even more ways to improve their diet, and possibly an invitation to come have dinner with the neighbors. Sometimes it's frustrating how even though I pass out Moringa seeds often, the women don't seem interested in growing their own trees. But when I think about it, all the trips to my trees keep me busy and provide opportunities to talk to people and experience more of the culture. The seeds will still be there after I leave, and maybe they will plant them later. For now, the visits are fun.

After noon it can get really hot in up-country Gambia. If it's too hot to work outside, there is always something to fix, write up, or work on inside. Another way to pass the time is to grab a spot on the local bantaba, a large wooden bench, and brew some attayah, a local tea, with the men. These bantaba trips can be anything from a quiet time to reflect on your day, to a loud and boisterous conversation with some of the elder men in town. Even in small villages, the men often listen to their short-wave radios and have many opinions on the topics being discussed. If the bantaba is empty, a walk in the bush can lead to some interesting finds, or bush-fruit picking with my host brothers will provide our family and friends with a tasty local treat. After the heat dies down there is usually a little time to get in a few more visits to villagers or gardens, and then it's back home to wash up before it gets dark.

Sunset transforms the village, as all the women who were out working and kids who were at school all day return home. Mandinkas, the ethnic group I live with, are known for their loudness, and the evenings are full of drumbeats, shouting conversations, laughter, and music. This is the best time to relax on my own and spend some time reading or writing letters to friends back home. In the cold season, to Gambians, a fire is always lit and sitting around sharing stories from America, or learning new proverbs and jokes in Mandinka can be another great way to get the most out of the day, even if there is no light.

Sometimes the days fly by, and sometimes they drag on and on, but each day has one thing in common--I know there will always be something new to learn from these people, or a new thing to do with my family and friends here. Trying to plan all my activities just won't work here, but if I just get involved and try to be a part of my community, the opportunities and adventures will come to me!

~ Dan Niebler, Health Volunteer

Maternal and child health (MCH) clinics are a great way to show your face around the village, get to know women, and share simple health messages and information. I consistently attended the five per month in my district, Niamina East, in lower Central River Division (CRD). MCH clinics are often dubbed "baby weighing" clinics among PCVs. And I did weigh babies! I also broke up fights between women trying to cut in line to get back to cooking lunch, checked immunization cards and recorded vaccinations given, got peed on, entered new births in the communities' log books, talked about breastfeeding, got peed on more, and counseled women on how to increase the nutrition in their children's diets. I drew aside women whose children's weights fell well below the average percentile for their age. In Wolof, we talked about locally available foods and how they can be incorporated into the compound's food bowl. Young babies can eat a pap (porridge) made from millet flour and beans, or oil or moringa powder can be added. Moringa can also be eaten in sauce or brewed like tea.

One of the MCH clinics was in a nearby Fula village where my communication with the women was limited because I couldn't speak the language. Most of the time clinics were understaffed and each of us filled two roles for the entire day. For this reason, it was difficult to pull my stubborn counterpart aside and have him translate into Fula my little spiel to women there. Eventually, he'd come and carefully translate to the woman a lesson about beans and moringa tea. He'd always tell me afterwards, "Roxi, please, we don't have time or enough people to talk to every woman individually in every village where we have a clinic!" Despite his frustrations I kept asking him to come and translate information for me when I couldn't do it on my own. Then, in my own village, Batti Njol, I heard him speaking to one of the women I had grown close to after a year there. He was talking about adding beans to pap and drying moringa for powder. He even used the same phrasing that I always did!

Even though it doesn't seem like a huge victory and we never spoke about it afterwards, it meant a lot to me to see that my counterpart had been listening to me for all those months. He was making the time to talk to my women about the health of their children.

~ Sara Hoffman, Health Volunteer, 2004-2007

Asalaamaa leekum! As you'll all hear plenty of times, "You are welcome!"

I'm an ICT specialist living about as far up-country as you can go in the hub city of Basse. I teach computers at a senior secondary school, and I'm staying busy with plenty of networking and database projects around the region at places such as the regional education office and the divisional health team office. The demand and need for trained computer users is ever increasing, and it's a rarity to find someone who doesn't want to learn more about computers and technology. Even if you're not an IT Volunteer, chances are you might end up being the computer expert at your place of work. Some of the non-IT projects I'm working on include a music club at my school and a regional art exhibit.

The cultural and geographic diversity in this tiny country may surprise you. Mansajang/Basse has both a city and village feel to it. For relaxation, I often ride my bike down to the river, or go hike some hills and enjoy the scenery. Everyone has their own unique experiences and opportunities and I hope you're ready to mold yours!

~ Evan Roth, Education Volunteer

Welcome to The Gambia.

I'm a math/science teacher stationed in Sintet, which is a village about 160 kilometers inland from the coast on the south bank. My village is on a bolang, and is surrounded by bush so it's nice to go for runs or bike rides and see a lot of wildlife with few people around. I've been teaching science to grades 8 and 9. In addition to teaching, some of the side projects I've been working on have been writing a science club guidebook that includes science experiments and activities using locally available resources, i.e. primarily recycled materials. Hopefully, I'll be able to distribute this book to all the lower and upper basic schools in the country. Other projects include tutoring, teaching at workshops for teachers, and instructing teachers on using the school library. I hope you are ready for a slower pace of life and yet a very wild two years in The Gambia.

~ Andrew Harris, Education Volunteer

Dear Future Peace Corps Volunteer,

First, I would like to welcome you to the Peace Corps/The Gambia program. The Peace Corps has been in The Gambia since 1967 and many dedicated Volunteers have served in its unique and diverse culture. This long-standing partnership demonstrates Peace Corps Volunteers' commitment to the development of The Gambia. You will now get to tell your friends and family, "I am moving to The Gambia, West Africa, and will spend the next two years volunteering there." I still get a smile saying it now.

I arrived over a year ago and now reside as a teacher-trainer in what we call the "up country" (which just means far from the capital). I work at the last of the six regional offices in a place called Basse. My work varies day-to-day, working at the office helping with anything from computer lessons, to teaching teachers how to use local materials in their classes. I am also helping a local nongovernmental organization in starting an orphanage in my village. In short, this is my service. I have spent the rest of my time making friends, going to celebrations, and sharing my life with the many Gambians I have contact with.

The Gambia is an amazing place to serve. Although I don't know where you will live or what language you will learn, I do know that you will find your service here as rewarding as I have. That's not to say that it's easy living here. Yes, we have great beaches and wonderful materials that you will design into your new fashion look, but it can be frustrating.

My advice to you is to remember what you want to get out of your service here. I truly believe that you will get out what you put in here. Your best asset is your failures, which you will inevitably learn from, and then adjusting your approach. And last, try to remain patient in your work, but always be persistent.

Good luck and enjoy this truly special program.

~ Ernie Herzig, Education Volunteer

PACKING LIST

This list has been compiled by Volunteers serving in Gambia and is based on their experience. Use it as an informal guide in making your own list, bearing in mind that each experience is individual. There is no perfect list! You obviously cannot bring everything on the list, so consider those items that make the most sense to you personally and professionally. You can always have things sent to you later. As you decide what to bring, keep in mind that you have an 100-pound weight limit on baggage. And remember, you can get almost everything you need in Gambia.

What to pack? How much stuff to take? What is available in The Gambia? How do I pack for two years? These are questions you are probably asking yourself right now; so this packing list has been created by Volunteers of Peace Corps/The Gambia (TG) to help give you an idea of what you need to bring and what can be found here. The packing list has been created by Volunteers and trainees to reflect the actual needs of Volunteers and is the most updated list for PC/TG. However, be advised that no one person will need everything on the list--be very selective. Only bring what you think you will use and use this list only as a guideline. There is absolutely nothing anyone can recommend for you to bring without which you will not be able to function as a Volunteer. People have shown up to The Gambia with nothing but a hiking backpack packed with a few clothes and toiletries and survived for 27 months. What you bring comes down to how you think you will live and how you want to live. The Peace Corps will provide all medicines and first aid necessities, as well as a cost of living (COL) allowance that will be enough for you to live comfortably. You can buy clothes or have clothes made by local tailors; you can buy almost all types of foods and toiletries you will ever need in-country. That being said, if you can bring some of the "luxury" things listed below, it will only help you. Furthermore, you do not HAVE to bring everything that you want with you. Almost everything on this list can be mailed to yourself, c/o the Peace Corps office in The Gambia, a week or two before you leave the U.S.(although it will not be cheap to do so), or you can arrange for family and friends to mail things to you later, after you have a better idea of what your needs will be.

Your address during your entire service will be the following:

> Your Name, PCT*
> C/O Peace Corps/The Gambia
> P.O. Box 582
> Banjul, The Gambia
> West Africa

*It is very important that you put PCT after your name (while you are in PST) or your mail may get misplaced. After you swear in as a Volunteer, PCV will follow your name.

Finally, items with an asterisk (*) are available in The Gambia; however, they may be low-quality, not your preferred brand, or may be too expensive for the average Volunteer budget.

General Clothing

Most Volunteers say they brought too much clothing, and in particular, too much "nice" clothing. Nevertheless, you will need to dress appropriately for meetings with government officials and for an occasional ceremony. But day to day, you will probably be living and working in a rural village in very hot weather.

Notes for Everyone on Clothing:

- Light-colored clothes are hard to keep clean. Dark clothes make you very hot, so you have to find a good balance. Brown, green, blue, gray, purple, and red, are good.
- The dress clothes for staging should be clothes you will wear in-country. In other words, don't bring specific clothes just for staging.

Women

The Gambia is a conservative Muslim country. Women usually cover all of their body, and many still cover their necks and heads. To dress in what Americans would consider warm-weather clothing may be considered by many Gambians to be provocative clothing, inviting more unwelcome attention than you will find tolerable. It is recommended that you err on the conservative side when choosing what clothes to bring.

Professional:

- Dresses (sundresses) are simple, culturally appropriate, and provide better ventilation than clothes with elastic waist bands. All skirts and pants should be three-fourth length (Capri or calf length) at a minimum. It is not culturally appropriate to show knees, but capri and calf-length pants are short enough not to drag in the mud or catch in bike spokes.
- Pants with belt loops, wrap tops, anything with forgiving fabric to accommodate fluctuations in weight.
- Keep in mind that tailors in the kombos (city areas) are good and fabrics are available for cheap custom tailoring (a dress costs about $10 USD), so the best advice is to pack minimal and versatile items and then supplement your wardrobe after receiving your assignment. Local tailors work well from patterns and excel at copying clothing you bring from home or show them in clothing catalogs.

Village Attire:

- Should be comfortable.
- Clothes get dirty, so bring clothes that can be washed frequently without falling apart. Clothes here take a beating since they are washed by hand.
- Bring lots of underwear! 20 pairs or more.*

- Bring at least several sports bras (quick-drying, cotton material is best.) Dark colors are easiest to keep clean looking.
- Pajamas–lightweight covering, light-colored to protect against mosquitoes (for sitting outside with host family/walking around village at night). Boxer shorts (more comfortable PJ's for sleeping at other Volunteers' houses or Peace Corps' transit house).

Kombo (City) Clothing:

- Bring a few outfits for potentially going out–there are opportunities to go dancing and occasions to feel pretty! Jeans, travel-sized toiletry bottles, disposable razors, two swimsuits (bikinis can be appropriate, but only at some of the tourist hotels; The Gambia caters to European tourists at beach resorts.)

Men

General:

- At least a couple of button-up dress shirts, preferably three or four
- T-Shirts*
- Long but light pants (since it gets hot here)
- Shorts (must cover knees)
- Underwear* (15 pairs or more)
- Pants that zip off into shorts can be very helpful and considered professional attire
- A few warmer shirts/ tops/ fleeces for "cold" season
- Swimsuit (shorts)

Kombo (city) clothing:

- A couple of changes of dressy clothes will come in handy for going out and attending official functions. (Meaning long sleeve button-up shirts with slacks or jeans).

Village Attire:

- Rule of thumb is don't show knees and you are perfectly fine. However, if you happen to be teaching in a class or working at a clinic or any other professional organization then you will need to dress more formally. Generally T-shirts and jeans can be considered appropriate for day-to-day village work, but in a classroom you will want a button-up shirt and slacks.

Shoes

- Flip-flops* (high-quality, for example, Haivaina or Teva; you can buy cheap flip-flops in-country)
- Sturdy sandals (Teva, Birkenstock, and Chaco are good brands)
- All-purpose shoes for walking, hiking, and biking (tennis shoes)*
- Workout shoes, if needed

Personal Hygiene and Toiletry Items

- Good scissors*
- Tweezers
- A good razor
- Skin lotion*
- Any favorite brands of shampoo, shaving cream, toothpaste, etc. (you can buy all of these things in-country at a cost)
- Deodorant (there is a very limited selection and it is very expensive so bring enough to last two years)*
- Lip balm (provided in the Peace Corps medical kit, but you may prefer your own brand)*
- Face wash/skin care products (e.g., Noxzema, Oxi pads, astringent)
- Talcum powder (e.g., Gold Bond, Summer's Eve) for heat rash
- Loofah(s) (a type of sponge)
- Sunscreen/bug spray (available from the PC medical office but it may not be the brand you like)
- Hand-sanitizer (bring lots and in many different sizes)
- Tampons (available from the PC medical office but if you have a favorite brand, bring some)
- Soap box
- Nail polish and remover

Work

- Calendar*
- Appointment book*
- Folders with pockets*
- Pens*
- Journal*
- Art supplies (markers, paper, colored pencils and sharpener)* *
- Note cards
- Women's magazines--good inspiration for women's group activities and products
- Voice recorder for language classes and mailing home tapes (Devices are available that make an iPod into a voice recorder as well)

- Teacher kit (For example, rubber bands, stapler, markers, Mr. Sketch, Sharpies, push pins, paper clips, pens, pencils, glue, single hole punch, and folders. Don't skimp-- really think about what you will want for the next two years.)
- Teaching materials (e.g., inflatable globes, electronic copies of lesson plans or resources, favorite teaching books, calculator, children's books that can be translated. Again, don't skimp.)

Kitchen

- Multivitamins and fiber supplements are available from the medical office. Consider bringing anything to supplement protein.
- Packaged mixes (Power aid/Gatorade, flavor drink mixes, powder soup mixes)
- Good can opener
- Small plastic food container(s), Tupperware (high-quality, you can store other things in these as well)*
- Favorite spices*
- Measuring cups and spoons
- Rubber spatula
- Plastic Ziploc bags
- Parmesan cheese (grated and packaged; it's very expensive here, so if you like it, bring your own)
- Dried fruit, raisins, Craisins, anything with nutrients
- Freeze-dried food
- Cliff bars or other energy bars (you cannot buy these in The Gambia and there may be times you may be stuck somewhere with little food options)
- Granola bars/protein bars
- Tuna, chicken and salmon packets
- Small Rubbermaid bins
- Pot holders
- Vegetable peeler
- Good knife*
- Travel mug*
- Diamond Stone/knife sharpener

Miscellaneous

- Portable solar power battery charger (these are expensive but very useful here; you can charge your MP3 player, cellphone, and rechargeable batteries. It is worth the money), and/or battery powered phone charger (for those times when there is no sun and/or you can't get to a town with electricity)
- Short-wave radio for listening to BBC, VOA, and other news stations*
- Converter for plugs (the one that comes with all of the options; The Gambia uses the British-type three-pronged plug)*

- Surge protectors*
- Small battery-operated fan
- Things to pass the time (e.g., long books on an iPod or in hard copy, Sudoko, crossword puzzles, etc. if you enjoy them)
- Small gifts for family if you want, but $10 or less (for example, stickers, postcards, extra pictures of your American family, crayons, markers, or pencils). (You do not have to buy anything in the U.S.; when you arrive in-country you will be taken to the market to get some cultural gifts for your host family.)
- Biking gear such as gloves, toe clips, bike seat for comfort (helmets and repair tools are provided by the Peace Corps. You may be biking a lot so these items are useful.)
- Water bottle
- Small or medium-size daypack without frame
- Disposable camera for times when you don't want to risk taking your digital camera
- Extra memory cards for your digital camera
- Film if you bring a nondigital camera (film is available in The Gambia, but is expensive and not the best quality)*
- U.S. stamps (for mailing letters with people traveling to the United States)
- Magazines and catalogs with pictures of clothing you might want to have copied by tailors in The Gambia
- Softball glove (Peace Corps/Senegal has an annual softball tournament with other West African countries)
- Plant and animal identification books (There are also many of these types of books floating around the office, the transit house, and with Volunteers)
- Protective cases for everything! (The dust and heat will kill your electronics if not in a case)
- Rechargeable batteries and recharger
- Blank CDs with cases (for burning pictures)*
- Bungie cords*
- Many types of tape (scotch, masking) *
- Sheet sack (fold and sew a queen-sized sheet up the side, making a sleeping sack for those times when you have to sleep somewhere you did not expect to)
- Bags (You can't have enough bags. Here are some suggestions: nylon drawstring, reusable canvas bag, book bag/backpack, daypack, duffel bags)
- Small two-person tent (nice for traveling and sleeping outside and in the bush)
- Sleeping pad for tent
- Clothesline and clothespins

Things you should bring

- Two pairs of flat bed sheets--queen size at least
- Two pillow cases
- Good towels* (bath towel, hand towels, and washcloth)

- Spoon, fork, and table knife (be sure to pack this in your checked luggage and NOT in your carry-on(s)
- At least a six-month supply of any prescription drugs you are currently taking (at least to last you until the medical office can order refills)
- Two pairs of eyeglasses, if you wear them; also consider bringing a repair kit
- A good can opener (good ones are NOT available in-country)

Extra things you will be glad you brought

- Cell phone with a SIM-card compatible with West Africa GSM frequencies ("quad band phone, unlocked" is the spec)*
- Flash drive(s) with large storage capacity (highly recommended)*
- A flashlight (one that charges by shaking is best), and/or headlamp
- Digital camera
- Duct tape
- Leatherman
- Sunglasses
- A phone card to call the U.S. from The Gambia more cheaply (available online)
- Africa map
- Mid-sized backpack
- Shoulder bag*
- Inexpensive, durable, water-resistant watch with extra batteries
- Wide-brimmed sun hat (useful for walking around town and particularly for working in the fields)
- Rain jacket
- Compact umbrella*
- iPod/CD player with choice of music
- Travel speakers
- Large combination lock and/or combination padlock
- ATM card
- Flyswatter
- Nalgene bottles (one wide-mouthed, one small)
- A mechanical or battery-operated alarm clock
- A small stockpile of rechargeable batteries (available in-country, but expensive)
- Bandanas
- A couple of small screw-top plastic containers/bottles for toiletries when traveling
- Toothbrush containers
- Photo album from home with photos of family/friends to share
- Good-quality pillow!*
- Earplugs (good ones with a high noise reduction rating is recommended)
- Collapsible hand fan
- A small (thin) blanket (it gets cold but never too cold)*

PRE-DEPARTURE CHECKLIST

The following list consists of suggestions for you to consider as you prepare to live outside the United States for two years. Not all items will be relevant to everyone, and the list does not include everything you should make arrangements for.

Family

- Notify family that they can call the Peace Corps' Counseling and Outreach Unit at any time if there is a critical illness or death of a family member (24-hour telephone number: 1-855-855-1961, then press 2; or directly at 202-692-1470).

- Give the Peace Corps' On the Home Front handbook to family and friends.

Passport/Travel

- Forward to the Peace Corps travel office all paperwork for the Peace Corps passport and visas.

- Verify that your luggage meets the size and weight limits for international travel.

- Obtain a personal passport if you plan to travel after your service ends. (Your Peace Corps passport will expire three months after you finish your service, so if you plan to travel longer, you will need a regular passport.)

Medical/Health

- Complete any needed dental and medical work.

- If you wear glasses, bring two pairs.

- Arrange to bring a three-month supply of all medications (including birth control pills) you are currently taking.

Insurance

- Make arrangements to maintain life insurance coverage.

- Arrange to maintain supplemental health coverage while you are away. (Even though the Peace Corps is responsible for your health care during Peace Corps service overseas, it is advisable for people who have pre-existing conditions to arrange for the continuation of their supplemental health coverage. If there is a lapse in coverage, it is often difficult and expensive to be reinstated.)

- Arrange to continue Medicare coverage if applicable.

Personal Papers

- Bring a copy of your certificate of marriage or divorce.

Voting

- Register to vote in the state of your home of record. (Many state universities consider voting and payment of state taxes as evidence of residence in that state.)

- Obtain a voter registration card and take it with you overseas.

- Arrange to have an absentee ballot forwarded to you overseas.

Personal Effects

- Purchase personal property insurance to extend from the time you leave your home for service overseas until the time you complete your service and return to the United States.

Financial Management

- Keep a bank account in your name in the U.S.

- Obtain student loan deferment forms from the lender or loan service.

- Execute a Power of Attorney for the management of your property and business.

- Arrange for deductions from your readjustment allowance to pay alimony, child support, and other debts through the Office of Volunteer Financial Operations at 855.855.1961, extension 1770.

- Place all important papers—mortgages, deeds, stocks, and bonds—in a safe deposit box or with an attorney or other caretaker.

CONTACTING PEACE CORPS HEADQUARTERS

This list of numbers will help connect you with the appropriate office at Peace Corps headquarters to answer various questions. You can use the toll-free number and extension or dial directly using the local numbers provided. Be sure to leave the toll-free number and extensions with your family so they can contact you in the event of an emergency.

Peace Corps Headquarters Toll-free Number: 855.855.1961, Press 1 or ext. # (see below)

Peace Corps' Mailing Address:

Peace Corps Headquarters
1111 20th Street, NW
Washington, DC 20526

Questions About:	Staff:	Toll-Free Ext:	Direct/Local #:
Responding to an Invitation	Office of Placement	x1840	202.692.1840
Country Information	Abdul Bala Desk Officer / (Senegal, The Gambia and Cape Verde) thegambia@peacecorps.gov	X2307	202.692.2307
Plane Tickets, Passports, Visas, or other travel matters:	CWT SATO Travel	x1170	202.692.1170
Legal Clearance	Office of Placement	x1840	202.692.1840
Medical Clearance & Forms Processing (includes dental)	Screening Nurse	x1500	202.692.1500
Medical Reimbursements (handled by a subcontractor)	Seven Corners	N/A	202.692.1538 800.335.0611
Loan Deferments, Taxes, Financial Operations	Office Of Volunteer and PSC Financial Services	x1770	202.692.1770
Readjustment Allowance Withdrawals, Power of Attorney, Staging (Pre-Departure Orientation), and Reporting Instructions	Office of Staging *Note: You will receive comprehensive information (hotel and flight arrangements) three to five weeks prior to departure. This information is not available sooner.*	x1865	202.692.1865
Family Emergencies (to get information to a Volunteer overseas) 24 hours	Office of Special Services	x1470	202.692.1470

www.ingramcontent.com/pod-product-compliance
Lightning Source LLC
Chambersburg PA
CBHW081749280526

45789CB00008B/2789

* 9 7 8 1 5 0 1 0 2 5 0 3 7 *